Rookie
Read-About® Science

You Can Use a Balance

By Linda Bullock

Consultants
David Larwa
National Science Consultant

Nanci R. Vargus, Ed.D.
Assistant Professor of Literacy
University of Indianapolis
Indianapolis, Indiana

Children's Press®
A Division of Scholastic Inc.
New York   Toronto   London   Auckland   Sydney
Mexico City   New Delhi   Hong Kong
Danbury, Connecticut

Designer: Herman Adler Design
Photo Researcher: Caroline Anderson
The photo on the cover shows a girl using a balance.

Library of Congress Cataloging-in-Publication Data

Bullock, Linda.
  You can use a balance / by Linda Bullock.
     p. cm. – (Rookie read-about science)
Includes index.
Summary: Simple text and photographs describe and illustrate the use of
a balance to measure or compare weights.
  ISBN 0-516-22869-2 (lib. bdg.)   0-516-27899-1 (pbk.)
  1. Balances (Weighing instruments)–Juvenile literature. [1. Balances
(Weighing instruments) 2. Weights and measures.] I. Title. II. Series.
  QC107.B85 2003
  681'.2–dc21
                            2003000468

CHILDREN'S PRESS, and ROOKIE READ-ABOUT®,
and associated logos are trademarks and or registered trademarks
of Scholastic Library Publishing. SCHOLASTIC and associated logos
are trademarks and or registered trademarks of Scholastic Inc.

17 18 R 22 21   62

Scholastic Inc., 557 Broadway, New York, NY 10012.

Come one, come all!

Help me balance
(BAL-uhns) the seesaw!
I will sit on this end.
You can sit on that end.

Oh, no! I am sorry.
You will not work.
You are too small!

Oh, no! I am sorry.
You will not work!
You are too big!

I need someone my size.

A seesaw is like a balance.

A balance is a tool that
tells which of two things
is heavier (HEV-ee-ur).
A simple balance has
two pans on a bar.

A seesaw moves up and
down. So does the bar on
a balance.

The side that is heavier goes down.

Let's see how a balance works.

Put some jelly beans in one of the pans on the balance. The pan with the jelly beans goes down. The empty pan goes up.

Now put gummy bears
in the other pan until the
pointer in the middle points
straight down.

Which side is heavier now?
They are both the same!

There are many different kinds of balances.

Some balances can tell you
how heavy something is.
Many kinds of balances
are used in markets.

Scientists (SYE-uhn-tists) use balances.

Jewelers use balances.

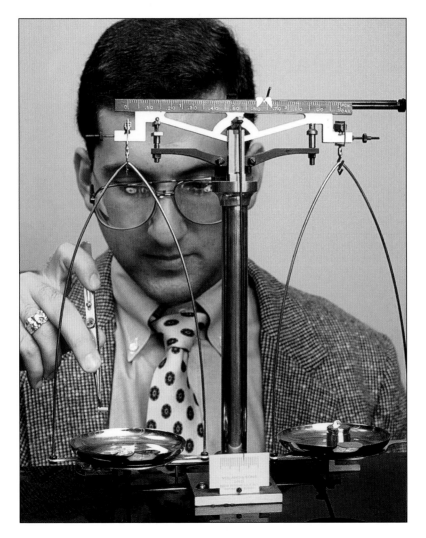

Some balances can measure (MEZH-uhr) things as big as a bear.

Some can measure things
as small as a bug.

Others can measure
things as big as you.

What could you measure
with your balance at a circus?
The elephant is too big.

The monkey is too big.

These monkeys and
elephants are not too big!

29

Words You Know

balance

elephant

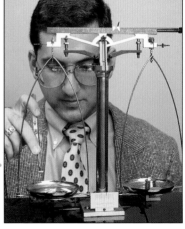

jeweler

monkey   scientist

seesaw

31

Index

About the Author

Dr. Linda Bullock lives in Austin, Texas, where she works as a writer and editor. She needs a very big balance to measure Phoebe, her Airedale terrier.

Photo Credits

Photographs © 2003: AP/Wide World Photos/Richard Vogel: 27, 31 top left; Corbis Images/AFP: 26, 30 bottom left; Ellen B. Senisi: 3, 5; Getty Images: 9; Photo Researchers, NY: 13 (Tim Davis), 20, 31 top right (David Leah/SPL), 22 (Joe Rychetnik); PhotoEdit: 12, 31 bottom (Spencer Grant), 23 (Will Hart), 25 (Michael Newman); Randy Matusow: cover, 15, 16, 29; The Image Bank/Getty Images/G.K. & Vikki Hart: 6; The Image Works: 21, 30 bottom right (Bob Daemmrich), 18 (Karen Preuss), 10, 30 top (Joseph Sohm), 19 (Syracuse Newspapers).